What Do Birds Eat?

All birds eat.

3

Songbirds eat **seeds** and grains.

seeds

Owls eat small animals.

Run, little mouse!

mouse

Robins eat worms.

They feed their babies in a **nest**.

nest

9

A pelican eats fish.

It uses its big **bill** to catch them.

bill

Hummingbirds eat flower **nectar**.

nectar

Nectar is sweet.

13

Did you find these words?

It uses its big **bill** to catch them.

Hummingbirds eat flower **nectar**.

They feed their babies in a **nest**.

Songbirds eat **seeds** and grains.

Photo Glossary

 **bill** (bil): The beak or jaw of a bird.

 **nectar** (nek-tur): A sweet liquid from flowers.

 **nest** (nest): A place built by birds and other small creatures to live in and take care of their young.

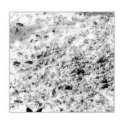 **seeds** (seeds): The parts of a flowering plant from which a new plant can grow.

Index

hummingbirds 12

owls 6

pelican 10

robins 8

songbirds 4

worms 8

About the Author

Savina Collins lives in Florida with her husband and five adventurous kids. Savina enjoys watching her kids surf and the pelicans dive for fish!

www.rourkeeducationalmedia.com

PHOTO CREDITS: Cover: ©Spondylolithesis (bird), ©valio84sl (seed); p.3: ©PrinPrince; p.2,4-5,14,15: ©KellyNelson; p.6-7: ©Lynn_Bystrom; p.2,8-9,14,15: ©Frank Paul/Alamy Stock Photo; p.2,10-11,14,15: ©Vadim Petrakov; p.2,12-13,14,15: ©InVision_Photography

Edited by: Keli Sipperley
Cover and interior design by: Rhea Magaro-Wallace

Library of Congress PCN Data
What Do Birds Eat? / Savina Collins
(Plants, Animals, and People)
ISBN (hard cover)(alk. paper) 978-1-64156-155-6
ISBN (soft cover) 978-1-64156-211-9
ISBN (e-Book) 978-1-64156-266-9
Library of Congress Control Number: 2017957767

Printed in the United States of America
01-3472111937